HANNAH, ARE YOU LISTENING?

HAMISH WHYTE

HAPPENSTANCE

Poems © Hamish Whyte, 2013
Cover image © Gillian Rose, 2013
ISBN 978-1-905939-95-4
All rights reserved.

Acknowledgements:
A version of 'A Letter to my Long-Lost Uncle' previously appeared in
New Writing Scotland 31 (Association for Scottish Literary Studies, 2013)

By the same author:
The Unswung Axe, Shoestring Press, 2012
A Bird in the Hand, Shoestring Press, 2008
Window on the Garden, Essence Press/Botanic Press, 2006
Siva in Lamlash, minimal missive, 1991
Rooms, Aquila Press, 1986
apple on an orange day, Autolycus Press, 1973

Printed by The Dolphin Press
www.dolphinpress.co.uk

Published in 2013 by Happen*Stance,*
21 Hatton Green, Glenrothes, Fife KY7 4SD
nell@happenstancepress.com
www.happenstancepress.com

CONTENTS

First and Last Swan / 5
Child Care / 6
Scaffold / 7
Five Stages / 8
New Clothes / 9
That Weekend We Forgot About the Dog / 10
49 Northumberland Street / 11
Reception / 12
Debt / 13
A Letter to my Long-Lost Uncle / 14
Hannah, are you listening? / 15
Keeping Watch / 16
One of Those Lives / 17
Ferry to Itea / 18
The Giraffe in Our Living-Room / 19
Moonshine with a Little Lemon / 20
My Castle / 21
Angus, did you ask? / 22
Desserts / 23
First Born / 24
Part of the Dance / 25
Before / 26
Long Afternoons / 27
What the Editor Said / 28

*For Diana with love
and thanks for the titles*

FIRST AND LAST SWAN

First swan I remember
was a match.

This one, patrolling
the same short stretch
of river is alone.
I can't tell whether
cob or pen, suspect
it's been widowed.

It has space to fly away
but chooses to stay.

It preens, it pokes
at the sedge,
sometimes chummed by one
or two ducks.
The heron paid
a visit but kept
its distance.

You want to save it
but from what?
Is it not a swan's job
just to be, to be there,
light against the dark?

CHILD CARE

Mention the children's playpark
and you picture it by Brueghel or Bosch:
little bodies ruined by fiendish torture machines,
heads split open, hangings from rigging,
falls from the top of a slide, falls from the side
of a slide, arms broken, legs smashed.
You dread grandson and granddaughter
shouting *Yes! Let's go to the playpark*:
dread dread dread and the what-if blame—
oh the scope for losing them.
Charades? you suggest,
knowing there's no escape from their urge to run,
climb things, stick their noddles through holes.
Love them, love their danger.

SCAFFOLD

Any scaffold's a dangerous
construction.

These four men as they climb
two storeys to the roof
are so practised they hook
us like circus performers.

They're so relaxed they can afford
to be daft: one hangs over
and swings his arm like a monkey;
one leans nonchalantly rolling
a cigarette.

A piece of planking floats upwards
like an Indian club, casually
caught with one hand by the man
at the top, the only one without
a hard hat, the one who slots the poles
in the holes with unfailing
accuracy.

There's a moment of rest; they pose
one above the other as if for
an illustration in a picture book.
They've reached that pinnacle
of art, making the difficult look
easy-peasy.

FIVE STAGES

innuendo
crescendo

        aggression
        possession

mystery   lager
history   stagger

        love
        above

NEW CLOTHES

in your nothings
in the changing-room
in the mirrors

you see what the emperor saw and the wee boy
you're a portrait by Lucian Freud
you're a piece of bacon by Bacon
you're what your eyes slip away from in the bathroom

is this you?
do you believe what the swindlers tell you?
look good feel good?

it's the natural stuffs you like
the feel of wool cotton silk makes you feel better
what you want is comfort with style
your own sexiness
a shape you can live with with a bit of show-off

the difference a hat makes

THAT WEEKEND WE FORGOT ABOUT THE DOG

We were entirely unBritished
by love and lust.
We writhed on the sheets
on the carpet
anywhere that took a back
or a front or hands and feet.

The dog was too good-mannered
to disturb us.
How it got into the fridge
and fed itself
we never found out.

When we came to
on Monday morning
the dog was sitting quietly
at the back door

eyes bright
and ready to run.

49 NORTHUMBERLAND STREET

I pass it every day
on my way to work:
the blinds are always drawn,
leaves collect on the doorstep.
I'm sure I once heard bagpipes playing
but it may have been a trick of the fog:
the fog's the only thing that seems to give it life
as if it draws the darkness inside into its own thickening
                                      and into our dreams.
I dream about it all the time
and when I wake I'm standing outside
and I know if I want to live
I must keep my bowler hat on
and knock at the door of 49 Northumberland Street
with my umbrella.

RECEPTION

It looked like the flophouse from hell.
I dinged the bell.
A woman appeared, her clothes too tight.
I need a room for the night,
I said. She said, *Let me see,*
I can give you twenty three
Front.
      Sounds good to me,
I said, taking the key.

So, window cracked open for air,
I sit waiting in a straight-backed chair.
They'll come for me, I know they will.
I put the gun down on the sill.
I've a few moments before they pound the bell
And strafe this place to hell.

DEBT

The grandfathers are the ones to thank,
they're the ones who escaped hunger,
lack of land, a horse and cart existence
to become station master, photographer,
dealer in oil and anything;
and the grandmothers with them
making do and mending:
socks, manners, grammar.

My great-grandfather Berry, church beadle,
late of the 11th Foot, died suddenly
in 1892, leaving his wife, a former mill girl,
with nine children in a Glasgow tenement.
There's a photograph of them all,
all immaculately turned out, heads up,
looking at their future.
One of them is my mother's father.

A LETTER TO MY LONG-LOST UNCLE

Why write now, when you're long gone?
Rummaging in the archive box the other day
I came across a photograph of you
in your ANZAC uniform, about 1915,
a sheepish grin memento.
My mother said you'd been an engineer
building Australia's roads and I imagined you,
tenement boy spooling into the outback.

That's what she was told. But now Aunt Myra,
your daughter, says not roads but railroads—
just a slight adjustment of romantic notioning:
you're still my grandpa's brother, great-uncle Sam,
who went off down under.
I have a picture and a story and that's enough
in a world that bleats *family family*,
that asks who do I think I am,
where Google knows nearly everything.

HANNAH, ARE YOU LISTENING?

It was a long time ago
and I was never on your radar
as we say now. Why you were
working in a library I'll never know
but it gave you, no-one's minion, plenty of scope
for saying yes and no
in the wrong places. I hope
you've still that sass and gall
I admired so much. After all
these years, remembering
your happy thrawnness, I just want to tell you,
long after you'd left, I did it too:

said no—to some mind-numbing
interminable catalogue-checking.
I wasn't punished; my stock
rose; for a while I was the talk
of the staff room: the man who said No
to Miss Smith. It's only a tiny chime
but I hope you hear it through ineluctable time.

KEEPING WATCH

Keeping watch outside and in
is the difficult thing
poets do, trying
not to, like falling
asleep with your eyes open.

ONE OF THOSE LIVES

One of those lives
that's more a tone of voice
than a biography.
No story,
no putting your finger on it.
Just a phrase someone said:
We loved to hear him laugh.

FERRY TO ITEA

A bunch of classics students seeing the sites
we waited on the Patrai quay in our clatty Bedford
minibus, *The Good the Bad and the Ugly*
echoing out over the water from someone's
boombox. The ferry threaded us
through the Gulf of Corinth—
yes, the wine-dark sea and honey light—
and on we went to Delphi
where there was no sybil to ask about the finals
but we drank from the Castalian spring
—water never so clear and cold.
In the amphitheatre I recited Homer
to test the acoustics.
The girls danced a can-can.

THE GIRAFFE IN OUR LIVING-ROOM

Possibly as strange to passing folk
as the one the Ming admiral brought back
to China in 1406, our giraffe
stands at the window in hat and scarf.
We call her Carmen, we talk to her, and
prefer her to any old elephant
in the room. She's that rare thing,
a listening creature who wisely says nothing.
Cheaper than a therapist,
more meditative than a Buddhist,
she embodies being and is-ness.
She looks out and in, and this
is her strength: maybe seeming odd at first sight,
she is—long neck, happy smile—just right.

MOONSHINE WITH A LITTLE LEMON

Deep in the pines
lost and you need a drink:
moonshine with a little lemon
will have to do.

The only rhyme
you find for *lemon*
is *demon* and it's for the eye
and has to do.

In any case
demon drink is what it is:
relax and blur
all you can do.

MY CASTLE

My castle is a bonfire
of autumn branches
that crack like gunshot;
woodsmoke catching
the throat.

My castle is a ruined priory
its stone stolen
to build a cliff-top fort.

My castle is tomorrow—
sun rising
on the unreachable beach.

ANGUS, DID YOU ASK?

My first day at work (forty-odd years ago)
you showed me round the library
from the gloomy basement and its ghost,
the strong room with its treasures
(smallest and largest book
and rarities in between)
to the fourth floor extension's view
of Minerva on her dome
and the joke about letting her away
for a tea break and the book hoist
down whose shaft Mr Blink's dentures fell
and the miles of mahogany shelves,
the million books and massed periodicals—

Angus, did you ask the question
I wanted to answer? No,
but the dust, the acid papery smell,
the five by three cards, the hint
of an index to everything
and thirty years of the great general public
did.

DESSERTS

We all get our puddings in the end.
Some are bread and butter.
Some are sticky toffee.
A lucky few get Eve's.
Gelato for the youngsters (scoops vary).
Fruit for the health-conscious.

Whether we deserve our desserts
is another matter—
who's to say?
Upside down
crisped with a blow torch
flamed with brandy—
a circle of hell
we'd all love to merry-go-round.

Or simply heavenly.

FIRST BORN

The dads were given
a few chairs on a landing.

I read *The Long Weekend*.

Heard the shout of *Forceps!*
along the corridor,
wasn't allowed in till afterwards:

two now three
in a tiny post-partum cubicle,
mother and father having the best
tea and toast of their lives.

PART OF THE DANCE

This part of the dance, swinging
round in the cruel Circassian Circle,
is where your knee goes *ping*.
You have to hobble
the rest, resist the atavistic urge to fling
women about—
and that's a good thing.

Maybe sitting out
is the best part of dancing,
watching the swirl,
mulling over old metaphors, the skirl
of life, etcetera:
or just nothing
much beyond *get me a lemonade from the bar*.

BEFORE

before
was when
was where
was how
was who
why was
after
what's the
puzzle

LONG AFTERNOONS

there's something going on
in the shadows
under the horse chestnut

but you're reluctant
to leave the safety
of your café chair and table

your notepad your book
your coffee
your arrangement

who you are today
and maybe tomorrow
if the weather holds

to go and see
what the scuffle is
the displacement—

just close your eyes
and put a squirrel to work
as the hours go by

WHAT THE EDITOR SAID

good idea well followed through we enjoyed
a great deal we read with pleasure and interest
there was much to take note of the bustle and
jar the excursion and homeward turn some
belters of poems got hold of my ears all well-
crafted precise rhyming we particularly liked
numbers three four and seven but